Dear Maggie
Just a little
remembrance for
you and the baby.
Wishing you and
your Mother a Merry
and happy Xmas. A.L.

To Maggie
    from

Mrs. Annie Lang
    Christmas 1911

CHRISTMAS

THE FEAST OF ST. FRIEND

THE FEAST
OF ST. FRIEND
A CHRISTMAS BOOK

BY
ARNOLD BENNETT
Author of "The Old Wives' Tale"
"Buried Alive", Etc., Etc.

New York
GEORGE H. DORAN
COMPANY

CONTENTS:

CHAPTER
ONE

THE FACT

ONE

THE FACT

SOMETHING has happened to Christmas, or to our hearts; or to both. In order to be convinced of this it is only necessary to compare the present with the past. In the old days of not so long ago the festival began to excite us in November. For weeks the house rustled with charming and thrilling secrets, and with the furtive noises of paper parcels being wrapped and unwrapped; the house was a whispering gallery. The tension of expectancy increased to such a point that there was a positive danger of the cord snapping before it ought to snap. On the Eve we went to bed with no hope of settled sleep. We knew that we should be wakened and kept awake by the waits singing in the cold; and we were glad to be kept awake so. On the supreme day we came downstairs hiding delicious yawns, and cordially pretending that we had never been more fit. The day was different from other days; it had a unique romantic quality, tonic, curative of all ills. On that day even the tooth-ache vanished, retiring far into the wilderness with the spiteful word, the venomous thought, and the unlovely gesture. We sang with gusto "Christians awake, salute the happy morn." We did salute the happy morn.

And when all the parcels were definitely unpacked, and the secrets of all hearts disclosed, we spent the rest of the happy morn in waiting, candidly

greedy, for the first of the great meals.
And then we ate, and we drank, and
we ate again; with no thought of nutri-
tion, nor of reasonableness, nor of the
morrow, nor of dyspepsia. We ate and
drank without fear and without shame,
in the sheer, abandoned ecstasy of celebration. And by means of motley
paper headgear, fit only for a carnival,
we disguised ourselves in the most absurd fashions, and yet did not make
ourselves seriously ridiculous; for ridi-
cule is in the vision, not in what is seen.
And we danced and sang and larked,
until we could no more. And finally
we chanted a song of ceremony, and
separated; ending the day as we had
commenced it, with salvoes of good
wishes. And the next morning we
were indisposed and enfeebled; and we
did not care; we suffered gladly; we

had our pain's worth, and more: This was the past.

*   *   *   *

Even today the spirit and rites of ancient Christmas are kept up, more or less in their full rigour and splendour, by a race of beings that is scattered over the whole earth. This race, mysterious, masterful, conservative, imaginative, passionately sincere, arriving from we know not where, dissolving before our eyes we know not how, has its way in spite of us. I mean the children. By virtue of the children's faith, the reindeer are still tramping the sky, and Christmas Day is still something above and beyond a day of the week; it is a day out of the week. We have to sit and pretend; and with disillusion in our souls we do pretend. At Christmas, it is not the

children who make-believe; it is ourselves. Who does not remember the
first inkling of a suspicion that Christmas Day was after all a day rather
like any other day? In the house of
my memories, it was the immemorial
duty of my brother on Christmas
morning, before anything else whatever happened, to sit down to the organ
and perform "Christians Awake" with
all possible stops drawn. He had to do
it. Tradition, and the will that ema-
nated from the best bedroom, combined
to force him to do it. One Christmas
morning, as he was preparing the stops,
he glanced aside at me with a supercili-
ous curl of the lips, and the curl of my
lips silently answered. It was as if
he had said: "I condescend to this," and
as if I had said: "So do I."

Such a moment comes to most of us

of this generation. And thenceforward the change in us is extraordinarily rapid. The next thing we know is that the institution of waits is a rather annoying survival which at once deprives us of sleep and takes money out of our pockets. And then Christmas is gluttony and indigestion and expensiveness and quarter-day, and Christmas cards are a tax and a nuisance, and present-giving is a heavier tax and a nuisance. And we feel self-conscious and foolish as we sing "Auld Lang Syne." And what a blessing it will be when the "festivities" (as they are misleadingly called) are over, and we can settle down into commonsense again!

* * * *

I do not mean that our hearts are black with despair on Christmas Day.

I do not mean that we do not enjoy ourselves on Christmas Day. There is no doubt that, with the inspiriting help of the mysterious race, and by the force of tradition, and by our own gift of pretending, we do still very much enjoy ourselves on Christmas Day. What I mean to insinuate, and to assert, is that beneath this enjoyment is the disconcerting and distressing conviction of unreality, of non-significance, of exaggerated and even false sentiment. What I mean is that we have to brace and force ourselves up to the enjoyment of Christmas. We have to induce deliberately the "Christmas feeling." We have to remind ourselves that "it will never do" to let the heartiness of Christmas be impaired. The peculiarity of our attitude towards Christmas, which at worst is a vacation, may be clearly seen by contrasting it with our attitude towards another vacation—the summer holiday. We do not have to brace and force ourselves up to the enjoyment of the summer holiday. We experience no difficulty in inducing the holiday feeling. There is no fear of the institution of the summer holiday losing its heartiness. Nor do we need the example of children to aid us in savouring the August "festivities."

*   *   *   *

If any person here breaks in with the statement that I am deceived and the truth is not in me, and that Christmas stands just where it did in the esteem of all right-minded people, and that he who casts a doubt on the heartiness of Christmas is not right-minded, let that person read no more. This book is not written for him. And if any other person, kindlier, condescendingly protests that there is nothing wrong with Christmas except my advancing age, let that person read no more. This book is not written for him, either. It is written for persons who can look facts cheerfully in the face. That Christmas has lost some of its magic is a fact that the common sense of the western hemisphere will not dispute. To blink the fact is infantile. To confront it, to try to understand it, to reckon with it, and to obviate any evil that may attach to it—this course alone is meet for an honest man.

CHAPTER
TWO

—

THE REASON

TWO

THE REASON

IF the decadence of Christmas were
a purely subjective phenomenon,
confined to the breasts of those of
us who have ceased to be children
then it follows that Christmas has
always been decadent, because people have always been ceasing to
be children. It follows also that the
festival was originally got up by disillusioned adults, for the benefit of the
children. Which is totally absurd.
Adults have never yet invented any institution, festival or diversion specially
for the benefit of children. The egoism
of adults makes such an effort impos-

sible, and the ingenuity and pliancy of children make it unnecessary. The pantomime, for example, which is now pre-eminently a diversion for children, was created by adults for the amusement of adults. Children have merely accepted it and appropriated it. Children, being helpless, are of course fatalists and imitators. They take what comes, and they do the best they can with it. And when they have made something their own that was adult, they stick to it like leeches.

They are terrific Tories, are children; they are even reactionary! They powerfully object to changes. What they most admire in a pantomime is the oldest part of it, the only true pantomime—the harlequinade! Hence the very nature of children is a proof that what Christmas is now to them, it was in the past to their elders. If they now feel and exhibit faith and enthusiasm in the practice of the festival, be sure that, at one time, adults felt and exhibited the same faith and enthusiasm —yea, and more! For in neither faith nor enthusiasm can a child compete with a convinced adult. No child could believe in anything as passionately as the modern millionaire believes in money, or as the modern social reformer believes in the virtue of Acts of Parliament.

Another and a crowning proof that Christmas has been diminished in our hearts lies in the fiery lyrical splendour of the old Christmas hymns. Those hymns were not written by people who made-believe at Christmas for the pleasure of youngsters. They were

written by devotees. And this age
could not have produced them.

* * * *

No! The decay of the old Christmas
spirit among adults is undeniable, and
its cause is fairly plain. It is due to the
labours of a set of idealists—men who
cared not for money, nor for glory, nor
for anything except their ideal. Their
ideal was to find out the truth concerning nature and concerning human history; and they sacrificed all—they sacrificed the peace of mind of whole generations—to the pleasure of slaking
their ardour for truth. For them the
most important thing in the world was
the satisfaction of their curiosity. They
would leave naught alone; and they
scorned consequences. Useless to cry
to them: "That is holy. Touch it not!"
I mean the great philosophers and men

of science—especially the geologists—
of the nineteenth century. I mean
such utterly pure-minded men as Lyell,
Spencer, Darwin and Huxley. They
inaugurated the mighty age of doubt
and scepticism. They made it impossible to believe all manner of things
which before them none had questioned.
The movement spread until uneasiness
was everywhere in the realm of thought,
and people walked about therein fear-
somely, as in a land subject to earth-
quakes. It was as if people had said:
"We don't know what will topple next.
Let's raze everything to the ground,
and then we shall feel safer." And
there came a moment after which nobody could ever look at a picture of the
Nativity in the old way. Pictures of
the Nativity were admired perhaps as
much as ever, but for the exquisite

beauty of their naïveté, the charm of
their old-world simplicity, not as artis-
tic renderings of fact.

*   *   *   *

An age of scepticism has its faults,
like any other age, though certain persons have pretended the contrary.
Having been compelled to abandon its
belief in various statements of alleged
fact, it lumps principles and ideals
with alleged facts, and hastily decides
not to believe in anything at all. It
gives up faith, it despises faith, in spite
of the warning of its greatest philosophers, including Herbert Spencer,
that faith of some sort is necessary to a
satisfactory existence in a universe full
of problems which science admits it can
never solve. None were humbler than
the foremost scientists about the nar-
rowness of the field of knowledge, as

compared with the immeasurability of
the field of faith. But the warning has
been ignored, as warnings nearly always are. Faith is at a discount. And
the qualities which go with faith are at
a discount; such as enthusiasm, spon-
taneity, ebullition, lyricism, and self-
expression in general. Sentimentality
is held in such horror that people are
afraid even of sentiment. Their secret
cry is: "Give us something in which
we can believe."

*   *   *   *

They forget, in their confusion, that
the great principles, spiritual and
moral, remain absolutely intact. They
forget that, after all the shattering discoveries of science and conclusions of
philosophy, mankind has still to live
with dignity amid hostile nature, and
in the presence of an unknowable

power and that mankind can only succeed in this tremendous feat by the exercise of faith and of that mutual goodwill which is based in sincerity and
charity. They forget that, while facts
are nothing, these principles are everything. And so, at that epoch of the
year which nature herself has ordained
for the formal recognition of the situation of mankind in the universe and of
its resulting duties to itself and to the
Unknown—at that epoch, they bewail,
sadly or impatiently or cynically: "Oh!
The bottom has been knocked out of
Christmas!"

*   *   *   *

But the bottom has not been knocked
out of Christmas. And people know it.
Somewhere, in the most central and
mysterious fastness of their hearts, they
know it. If they were not, in spite of
themselves, convinced of it, why

should they be so pathetically anxious to keep alive in themselves, and to foster in their children, the Christmas spirit? Obviously, a profound instinct is for ever reminding them that, without the Christmas spirit, they are lost. The forms of faith change, but the spirit of faith, which is the Christmas spirit, is immortal amid its endless vicissitudes. At a crisis of change, faith is weakened for the majority; for the majority it may seem to be dead. It is conserved, however, in the hearts of the few supremely great and in the hearts of the simple. The supremely great are hidden from the majority; but the simple are seen of all men, and them we encourage, often without knowing why, to be the depositaries of that which we cannot ourselves guard, but which we dimly feel to be indispensable to our safety.

CHAPTER
THREE

THE SOLSTICE
AND GOOD WILL

THREE

THE SOLSTICE AND GOOD WILL

IN order to see that there is under-
lying Christmas an idea of faith
which will at any rate last as long as
the planet lasts, it is only necessary to
ask and answer the question: "Why
was the Christmas feast fixed for the
twenty-fifth of December?" For it is
absolutely certain, and admitted by
everybody of knowledge, that Christ
was not born on the twenty-fifth of
December. Those disturbing impas-
sioned inquirers after truth, who will
not leave us peaceful in our ignorance,
have settled that for us, by pointing
out, among other things, that the

twenty-fifth of December falls in the
very midst of the Palestine rainy sea-
son, and that, therefore, shepherds were
assuredly not on that date watching
their flocks by night.

*   *   *   *

Christians were not, at first, united
in the celebration of Christmas. Some
kept Christmas in January, others in
April, others in May. It was a pre-
Christian force which drove them all
into agreement upon the twenty-fifth
of December. Just as they wisely took
the Christmas tree from the Roman
Saturnalia, so they took the date of
their festival from the universal pre-
Christian festival of the winter solstice,
Yule, when mankind celebrated the
triumph of the sun over the powers of
darkness, when the night begins to de-
crease and the day to increase, when

the year turns, and hope is born again
because the worst is over. No more
suitably symbolic moment could have
been chosen for a festival of faith, goodwill and joy. And the appositeness of
the moment is just as perfect in this era
of electric light and central heating, as
it was in the era of Virgil, who, by the
way, described a Christmas tree. We
shall say this year, with exactly the
same accents of relief and hope as our
pagan ancestors used, and as the
woaded savage used: "The days will
begin to lengthen now!" For, while
we often falsely fancy that we have
subjugated nature to our service, the
fact is that we are as irremediably as
ever at the mercy of nature.

*   *   *   *

Indeed, the attitude of us moderns
towards the forces by which our exist-

ence is governed ought to be, and probably is, more reverent and awe-struck than that of the earlier world. The discoveries of science have at once quickened our imagination and compelled us to admit that what we know is the merest trifle. The pagan in his ignorance explained everything. Our knowledge has only deepened the mystery, and all that we shall learn will but deepen it further. We can explain the solstice. We are aware with absolute certitude that the solstice and the equinox and the varying phenomena of the seasons are due to the fact that the plane of the equator is tilted at a slight angle to the plane of the ecliptic. When we put on the first overcoat in autumn, and when we give orders to let the furnace out in spring, we know that we are arranging our lives in accordance with that angle. And we are quite duly proud of our knowledge. And much good does our knowledge do us!

*   *   *   *

Well, it does do us some good, and in a spiritual way, too! For nobody can even toy with astronomy without picturing to himself, more clearly and startlingly than would be otherwise possible, a revolving globe that whizzes through elemental space around a ball of fire: which, in turn, is rushing with all its satellites at an inconceivable speed from nowhere to nowhere; and to the surface of the revolving, whizzing globe a multitude of living things desperately clinging, and these living things, in the midst of cataclysmic danger, and between the twin enigmas of birth and death, quarrelling and hating and calling themselves kings and queens and millionaires and beautiful women and aristocrats and geniuses and lackeys and superior persons! Perhaps the highest value of astronomy is that it renders more vivid the ironical significance of such a vision, and thus brings home to us the truth that in spite of all the differences which we have invented, mankind is a fellowship of brothers, overshadowed by insoluble and fearful mysteries, and dependent upon mutual goodwill and trust for the happiness it may hope to achieve. * * * Let us remember that Christmas is, among other things, the winter solstice, and that the bottom has not yet been knocked out of the winter solstice, nor is likely to be in the immediate future!

*   *   *   *

It is a curious fact that the one faith which really does flourish and wax in

these days should be faith in the idea of
social justice. For social justice simply means the putting into practice of
goodwill and the recognition of the
brotherhood of mankind. Formerly,
people were enthusiastic and altruistic
for a theological idea, for a national
idea, for a political idea. You could
see men on the rack for the sake of a
dogma; you could see men of a great
nation fitting out regiments and ruin-
ing themselves and going forth to save
a small nation from destruction. You
could see men giving their lives to the
aggrandisement of an empire. And
the men who did these things had the
best brains and the quickest wits and
the warmest hearts of their time. But
today, whenever you meet a first-class
man who is both enthusiastic and altruistic, you may be sure that his pet

scheme is neither theological, military nor political; you may be sure that he has got into his head the notion that some class of persons somewhere are not being treated fairly, are not being treated with fraternal goodwill, and that he is determined to put the matter right, or perish.

*   *   *   *

In England, nearly all the most interesting people are social reformers: and the only circles of society in which you are not bored, in which there is real conversation, are the circles of social reform. These people alone have an abounding and convincing faith. Their faith has, for example, convinced many of the best literary artists of the day, with the result that a large proportion of the best modern imaginative literature has been inspired by the dream of social justice. Take away that idea from the works of H. G. Wells, John Galsworthy and George Bernard Shaw, and there would be exactly nothing left. Despite any appearance to the contrary, therefore, the idea of universal goodwill is really alive upon the continents of this planet: more so, indeed, than any other idea—for the vitality of an idea depends far less on the numbers of people who hold it than on the quality of the heart and brain of the people who hold it. Whether the growth of the idea is due to the spiritual awe and humility which are the consequence of increased scientific knowledge, I cannot say, and I do not seriously care.

CHAPTER FOUR

THE APPOSITENESS OF CHRISTMAS

FOUR

THE APPOSITENESS OF CHRISTMAS

YES," you say, "I am quite at one with you as to the immense importance of goodwill in social existence, and I have the same faith in it as you have. But why a festival? Why eating and drinking and ceremonies? Surely one can have faith without festivals?"

*　　　*　　　*　　　*

The answer is that one cannot; or at least that in practice, one never does. A disinclination for festivals, a morbid self-conscious fear of letting oneself go, is a sure sign of lack of faith. If you have not enough enthusiasm for the

cult of goodwill to make you positively
desire to celebrate the cult, then your
faith is insufficient and needs fostering
by study and meditation. Why, if you
decide to found a sailing-club up your
creek, your very first thought is to sig-
nalise your faith in the sailing of those
particular waters by a dinner and a
jollity, and you take care that the
event shall be an annual one! * * *
You have faith in your wife, and in
your affection for her. Surely you
don't need a festival to remind you of
that faith, you so superior to human
weaknesses? But you do! You insist
on having it. And, if the festival did
not happen, you would feel gloomy
and discouraged. A birthday is a device for recalling to you in a formal
and impressive manner that a certain
person still lives and is in need of good-

will. It is a device which experience
has proved to be both valuable and
necessary.

* * * *

Real faith effervesces; it shoots forth
in every direction; it communicates itself. And the inevitable result is a festival. The festival is anticipated with
pleasure, and it is remembered with
pleasure. And thus it reacts stimulatingly on that which gave it birth, as the
vitality of children reacts stimulatingly
on the vitality of parents. It provides
a concrete symbol of that which is invisible and intangible, and mankind is
not yet so advanced in the path of
spiritual perfection that we can afford
to dispense with concrete symbols.
Now, if we maintain festivals and
formalities for the healthy continuance
and honour of a pastime or of a per-

sonal affection, shall we not maintain
a festival—and a mighty one—in be-
half of a faith which makes the corpor-
ate human existence bearable amid the
menaces and mysteries that for ever
threaten it,—the faith of universal
goodwill and mutual confidence?

*   *   *   *

If then, there is to be a festival, why
should it not be the festival of Christmas?   It can, indeed, be no other.
Christmas is most plainly indicated. It
is dignified and made precious by tra-
ditions which go back much further
than the Christian era; and it has this
tremendous advantage—it exists!   In
spite of our declining faith, it has been
preserved to us, and here it is, ready to
hand.   Not merely does it fall at the
point which uncounted generations
have agreed to consider as the turn of

the solar year and as the rebirth of
hope! It falls also immediately before
the end of the calendar year, and thus
prepares us for a fresh beginning that
shall put the old to shame. It could
not be better timed. Further, its tra-
ditional spirit of peace and goodwill is
the very spirit which we desire to foster. And finally its customs—or at
any rate, its main customs—are well
designed to symbolize that spirit. If
we have allowed the despatch of Christmas cards to degenerate into naught
but a tedious shuffling of paste-boards
and overwork of post-office officials,
the fault is not in the custom but in
ourselves. The custom is a most striking one—so long as we have sufficient
imagination to remember vividly that
we are all in the same boat—I mean,
on the same planet—and clinging des-

perately to the flying ball, and dependent for daily happiness on one another's good will! A Christmas card sent by one human being to another human being is more than a piece of coloured stationery sent by one log of wood to another log of wood: it is an inspiring and reassuring message of high value. The mischief is that so many self-styled human beings are just logs of wood, rather stylishly dressed.

* * * *

And then the custom of present-giving! What better and more convincing proof of sympathy than a gift? The gift is one of these obvious contrivances—like the wheel or the lever—which smooth and simplify earthly life, and the charm of whose utility no obviousness can stale. But of course any contrivance can be rendered futile by clumsiness or negligence. There is a sort of Christmas giver who says pettishly: "Oh! I don't know what to give to So-and-So this Christmas! What a bother! I shall write and tell her to choose something herself, and send the bill to me!" And he writes. And though he does not suspect it, what he really writes, and what So-and-So reads, is this: "Dear So-and-So. It is nothing to me that you and I are alive together on this planet, and in various ways mutually dependent. But I am bound by custom to give you a present. I do not, however, take sufficient interest in your life to know what object it would give you pleasure to possess; and I do not want to be put to the trouble of finding out, nor of obtaining the object and transmitting it to you. Will you, therefore, buy something for yourself and send the bill to me. Of course, a sense of social decency will prevent you from spending more than a small sum, and I shall be spared all exertion beyond signing a cheque. Yours insincerely and loggishly * * *." So managed, the contrivance of present-giving becomes positively sinister in its working. But managed with the sympathetic imagination which is infallibly produced by real faith in goodwill, its efficacy may approach the miraculous.

*   *   *   *

The Christmas ceremony of good-wishing by word of mouth has never been in any danger of falling into insincerity. Such is the power of tradition and virtue of a festival, and such the instinctive brotherliness of men, that on this day the mere sight of an

[44]

acquaintance will soften the voice and warm the heart of the most superior sceptic and curmudgeon that the age of disillusion has produced. In spite of himself, faith flickers up in him again, be it only for a moment. And, during that moment, he is almost like those whose bright faith the age has never tarnished, like the great and like the simple, to whom it is quite unnecessary to offer a defence and explanation of Christmas or to suggest the basis of a new faith therein.

CHAPTER
FIVE
—
DEFENCE OF FEASTING

FIVE

DEFENCE OF FEASTING

AND now I can hear the superior sceptic disdainfully questioning: "Yes, but what about the orgy of Christmas? What about all the eating and drinking?" To which I can only answer that faith causes effervescence, expansion, joy, and that joy has always, for excellent reasons, been connected with feasting. The very words 'feast' and 'festival' are etymologically inseparable. The meal is the most regular and the least dispensable of daily events; it happens also to be an event which is in itself almost invariably a source of pleasure, or, at worst, of satisfaction: and it will continue to have this precious quality so long as our souls are encased in bodies. What could be more natural, therefore, than that it should be employed, with due enlargement and ornamentation, as the kernel of the festival? What more logical than that the meal should be elevated into a feast?

"But," exclaims the superior sceptic, "this idea involves the idea of excess!" What if it does? I would not deny it! Assuredly, a feast means more than enough, and more than enough means excess. It is only because a feast means excess that it assists in the bringing about of expansion and joy. Such is human nature, and it is the case of human nature that we are discussing. Of course, excess usually exacts its toll, within twenty-four hours, especially from the weak. But the benefit is worth its price. The body pays no more than the debt which the soul has incurred. An occasional change of habit is essential to well-being, and every change of habit results in temporary derangement and inconvenience.

Do not misunderstand me. Do not push my notion of excess to extremes. When I defend the excess inevitably incident to a feast, I am not seeking to prove that a man in celebrating Christmas is entitled to drink champagne in a public restaurant until he becomes an object of scorn and disgust to the waiters who have travelled from Switzerland in order to receive his tips. Much less should I be prepared to justify him if, in his own home, he sank lower than the hog. Nor would I sympathetically carry him to bed. There is such a thing as excess in moderation and dignity. Every wise man has practised this. And he who has not practised it is a fool, and deserves even a harder name. He ought indeed to inhabit a planet himself, for all his faith in humanity will be exhausted in believing in himself. * * * So much for the feast!

*   *   *   *

But the accompaniments of the feast are also excessive. For example, you make a tug-of-war with your neighbour at table, and the rope is a fragile packet of tinselled paper, which breaks with a report like a pistol. You open your half of the packet, and discover some doggerel verse which you read aloud, and also a perfectly idiotic coloured cap, which you put on your head to the end of looking foolish. And this ceremony is continued until the whole table is surrounded by preposterous headgear, and doggerel verse is lying by every plate. Surely no man in his senses, no woman in hers, would, etc., etc. * * * ! But one of the spiritual advantages of feasting is that it expands you beyond your common sense. One excess induces another, and a finer one. This acceptance of the ridiculous is good for you. It is particularly good for an Anglo-Saxon, who is so self-contained and self-controlled that his soul might stiffen as the unused limb of an Indian fakir stiffens, were it not for periodical excitements like that of the Christmas feast. Everybody has experienced the self-conscious reluctance which precedes the putting on of the cap, and the relief,

followed by further expansion and
ecstasy, which ensues after the putting
on. Everybody who has put on a cap
is aware that it is a beneficial thing to
put on a cap. Quite apart from the
fact that the mysterious and fanciful
race of children are thereby placated
and appeased, the soul of the capped
one is purified by this charming excess.

*   *   *   *

And the Tree! What an excess of
the fantastic to pretend that all those
glittering balls, those coloured candles
and those variegated parcels are the
blossoms of the absurd tree! How ex-
cessively grotesque to tie all those parcels to the branches, in order to take
them off again! Surely, something less
mediæval, more ingenious, more modern than this could be devised—if symbolism is to be indulged in at all! Can

you devise it, O sceptical one, revelling
in disillusion? Can you invent a symbol more natural and graceful than the
symbol of the Tree? Perhaps you
would have a shop-counter, and shelves
behind it, so as to instil early into the
youthful mind that this is a planet of
commerce! Perhaps you would abolish
the doggerel of crackers, and substitute
therefor extracts from the Autobio-
graphy of Benjamin Franklin! Perhaps you would exchange the caps for
blazonry embroidered with chemical
formula, your object being the ad-
vancement of science! Perhaps you
would do away with the orgiastic eating and drinking, and arrange for a
formal conversation about astronomy
and the idea of human fraternity, upon
strictly reasonable rations of shredded
wheat! You would thus create an

original festival, and eliminate all fear of a dyspeptic morrow. You would improve the mind. And you would avoid the ridiculous. But also, in avoiding the ridiculous, you would tumble into the ridiculous, deeply and hopelessly! And think how your very original festival would delight the participators, how they would look forward to it with joy, and back upon it with pleasurable regret; how their minds would dwell sweetly upon the conception of shredded wheat, and how their faith would be encouraged and strengthened by the intellectuality of the formal conversation!

*　　　*　　　*　　　*

He who girds at an ancient established festival should reflect upon sundry obvious truths before he withers up the said festival by the sirocco of his contempt. These truths are as follows:—First, a festival, though based upon intelligence, is not an affair of the intellect, but an affair of the emotions. Second, the human soul can only be reached through the human body. Third, it is impossible to replace an ancient festival by a new one. Robespierre, amongst others, tried to do so, and achieved the absurd. Reformers, heralds of new faiths, and rejuvenators of old faiths, have always, when they succeeded, adopted an ancient festival, with all or most of its forms, and been content to breathe into it a new spirit to replace the old spirit which had vanished or was vanishing. Anybody who, persuaded that Christmas is not what it was, feels that a festival must nevertheless be preserved, will do well to follow this example. To be content with the old forms and to vitalize them: that is the problem. Solve it, and the forms will soon begin to adapt themselves to the process of vitalization. All history is a witness in proof.

CHAPTER
SIX

TO REVITALIZE
THE FESTIVAL

SIX

TO REVITALIZE THE FESTIVAL

IT being agreed, then, that the Christmas festival has lost a great deal of its old vitality, and that, to many people, it is a source of tedium and the cause of insincerity; and it being further agreed that the difficulty cannot be got over by simply abolishing the festival, as no one really wants it to be abolished; the question remains—what should be done to vitalize it? The former spirit of faith, the spirit which made the great Christmas of the golden days, has been weakened; but one element of it—that which is founded on the conviction that goodwill among men is a prime necessity of reasonable living—survives with a certain vigour, though even it has not escaped the general scepticism of the age. This element unites in agreement all the pugnacious sectaries who join battle over the other elements of the former faith. This element has no enemies. None will deny its lasting virtue. Obviously, therefore, the right course is to concentrate on the cultivation of goodwill. If goodwill can be consciously increased, the festival of Christmas will cease to be perfunctory. It will acquire a fresh and more genuine significance, which, however, will not in any way inconvenience those who have never let go of the older significance. No tradition will be overthrown, no shock administered, and nobody will be able to croak about iconoclasm and

new-fangled notions and the sudden
end of the world, and so on.

      *   *   *   *

The fancy of some people will at
once run to the formation of a grand
international Society for the revivify-
ing of Christmas by the cultivation of
goodwill, with branches in all the chief
cities of Europe and America, and
headquarters—of course at the Hague;
and committees and subcommittees,
and presidents and vice-presidents;
and honorary secretaries and secretaries paid; and quarterly and annual
meetings, and triennial congresses!
And a literary organ or two! And a
badge—naturally a badge, designed by
a famous artist in harmonious tints!

      *   *   *   *

But my fancy does not run at all in
this direction. I am convinced that we

have already far too many societies for
the furtherance of our ends. To my
mind, most societies with a moral aim
are merely clumsy machines for doing
simple jobs with the maximum of fric-
tion, expense and inefficiency. I should
define the majority of these societies as
a group of persons each of whom ex-
pects the others to do something very
wonderful. Why create a society in
order to help you to perform some act
which nobody can perform but yourself? No society can cultivate goodwill
in you. You might as well create a society for shaving or for saying your
prayers. And further, goodwill is far
less a process of performing acts than
a process of thinking thoughts. To
think, is it necessary to involve yourself in the cog-wheels of a society?
Moreover, a society means fuss and

shouting: two species of disturbance which are both futile and deleterious— particularly in an intimate affair of morals.

You can best help the general culti- vation of goodwill along by cultivating goodwill in your own heart. Until you have started the task of personal culti- vation, you will probably assume that there will be time left over for super- intending the cultivation of goodwill in other people's hearts. But a very little experience ought to show you that this is a delusion. You will perceive, if not at once, later, that you have bitten off just about as much as you can chew. And you will appreciate also the wis- dom of not advertising your enterprise. Why, indeed, should you breathe a word to a single soul concerning your admirable intentions? Rest assured that any unusual sprouting of the desired crop will be instantly noticed by the persons interested.

*　　　*　　　*　　　*

The next point is: Towards whom are you to cultivate goodwill? Naturally, one would answer: Towards the whole of humanity. But the whole of humanity, as far as you are concerned, amounts to naught but a magnificent abstract conception. And it is very difficult to cultivate goodwill towards a magnificent abstract conception. The object of goodwill ought to be clearly defined, and very visible to the physical eye, especially in the case of people, such as us, who are only just beginning to give to the cultivation of goodwill, perhaps, as much attention as we give to our clothes or our tobacco. If a novice sets out to embrace the whole of

humanity in his goodwill, he will have
even less success than a young man en-
deavouring to fall in love with four sis-
ters at once; and his daily companions
—those who see him eat his bacon and
lace his boots and earn his living—will
most certainly have a rough time of it.
* * * No! It will be best for you to
centre your efforts on quite a small
group of persons, and let the rest of
humanity struggle on as well as it can,
with no more of your goodwill than it
has hitherto had.

In choosing the small group of people, it will be unnecessary for you to go
to Timbuctoo, or into the next street or
into the next house. And, in this group
of people you will be wise, while neg-
lecting no member of the group, to
specialise on one member. Your wife,
if you have one, or your husband? Not

necessarily. I was meaning simply that one who most frequently annoys you. He may be your husband, or she may be your wife. These things happen. He may be your butler. Or you may be his butler. She may be your daughter, or he may be your father, and you a charming omniscient girl of seventeen wiser than anybody else. Whoever he or she may be who oftenest inspires you with a feeling of irritated superiority, aim at that person in particular.

The frequency of your early failures with him or her will show you how prudent you were not to make an attempt on the whole of humanity at once. And also you will see that you did well not to publish your excellent intentions. If nobody is aware of your striving, nobody will be aware that you have failed in striving. Your successes will appear effortless, and—most important of all—you will be free from the horrid curse of self-consciousness. Herein is one of the main advantages of not wearing a badge. Lastly, you will have the satisfaction of feeling that, if everybody else is doing as you are, the whole of humanity is being attended to after all. And the comforting thought is that very probably, almost certainly, quite a considerable number of people are in fact doing as you are; some of them—make no doubt—are doing a shade better. I now come to the actual method of cultivating goodwill.

CHAPTER
SEVEN

THE GIFT
OF ONESELF

SEVEN

THE GIFT OF ONESELF

CHILDREN divide their adult acquaintances into two categories—those who sympathise with them in the bizarre and trying adventure called life; and those who don't. The second category is much the larger of the two. Very many people belong to it who think that they belong to the first. They may deceive themselves, but they cannot deceive a child. Although you may easily practise upon the credulity of a child in matters of fact, you cannot cheat his moral and social judgment. He will add you up, and he will add anybody up, and he will estimate conduct, upon principles of his own and in a manner terribly impartial. Parents have no sterner nor more discerning critics than their own children.

And so you may be polite to a child, and pretend to appreciate his point of view; but, unless you really do put yourself to the trouble of understanding him, unless you throw yourself, by the exercise of imagination, into his world, you will not succeed in being his friend. To be his friend means an effort on your part, it means that you must divest yourself of your own mental habit, and, for the time being, adopt his. And no nice phrases, no gifts of money, sweets or toys, can take the place of this effort, and this sacrifice of self. With five minutes of genuine surrender to him, you can win more of his esteem and gratitude than five hundred pounds would buy. His notion of real goodwill is the imaginative sharing of his feelings, a convinced participation in his pains and pleasures. He is well aware that, if you honestly do this, you will be on his side.

* * * *

Now, adults, of course, are tremendously clever and accomplished persons and children are no match for them; but still, with all their talents and omniscience and power, adults seem to lack important pieces of knowledge which children possess; they seem to forget, and to fail to profit by, their infantile experience. Else why should adults in general be so extraordinarily ignorant of the great truth that the secret of goodwill lies in the sympathetic exercise of the imagination? Since goodwill is the secret of human happi-

ness, it follows that the secret of goodwill must be one of the most precious
aids to sensible living; and yet adults,
though they once knew it, have gone
and forgotten it! Children may well
be excused for concluding that the
ways of the adult, in their capricious ir-
rationality, are past finding out.

To increase your goodwill for a fellow creature, it is necessary to imagine
that you are he: and nothing else is
necessary. This feat is not easy; but
it can be done. Some people have less
of the divine faculty of imagination
than others, but nobody is without it,
and, like all other faculties, it improves
with use, just as it deteriorates with neglect. Imagination is a function of the
brain. In order to cultivate goodwill
for a person, you must think frequently about that person. You must in-

form yourself about all his activities. You must be able in your mind's eye to follow him hour by hour throughout the day, and you must ascertain if he sleeps well at night—because this is not a trifle. And you must reflect upon his existence with the same partiality as you reflect upon your own. (Why not?) That is to say, you must lay the fullest stress on his difficulties, disappointments and unhappinesses, and you must minimise his good fortune. You must magnify his efforts after righteousness, and forget his failures. You must ever remember that, after all, he is not to blame for the faults of his character, which faults, in his case as in yours, are due partly to heredity and partly to environment. And beyond everything you must always give him credit for good intentions. Do not you, though sometimes mistakenly, always act for the best? You know you do! And are you alone among mortals in rectitude?

* * * *

This mental exercise in relation to another person takes time, and it involves a fatiguing effort. I repeat that it is not easy. Nor is it invariably agreeable. You may, indeed, find it tedious, for example, to picture in vivid detail all the worries that have brought about your wife's exacerbation—negligent maid, dishonest tradesman, milk in a thunder storm, hypercritical husband, dirt in the wrong place—but, when you have faithfully done so, I absolutely defy you to speak to her in the same tone as you used to employ, and to cherish resentment against her as you used to do. And I absolutely

defy you not to feel less discontented
with yourself than in the past. It is
impossible that the exercise of imagination about a person should not result
in goodwill towards that person. The
exercise may put a strain upon you;
but its effect is a scientific certainty. It
is the supreme social exercise, for it is
the giving of oneself in the most intimate and complete sense. It is the sus-
pension of one's individuality in favour
of another. It establishes a new attitude of mind, which, though it may
well lead to specific social acts, is more
valuable than any specific act, for it is
ceaselessly translating itself into de-
meanour.

*   *   *   *

The critic with that terrible English
trait, an exaggerated sense of the ridiculous, will at this point probably re-

mark to himself, smiling: "I suppose the time will come, when by dint of regular daily practice, I shall have achieved perfect goodwill towards the first object of my attentions. I can then regard that person as 'done.' I can put him on a shelf, and turn to the next; and, in the end, all my relations, friends and acquaintances will be 'done' and I can stare at them in a row on the shelf of my mind, with pride and satisfaction * * * ." Except that no person will ever be quite "done," human nature, still being human, in spite of the recent advances of civilisation, I do not deprecate this manner of stating the case.

The ambitious and resolute man, with an exaggerated sense of the ridiculous, would see nothing ridiculous in ticking off a number of different objects as they were successively achieved. If for example it was part of his scheme to learn various foreign languages, he would know that he could only succeed by regular application of the brain, by concentration of thought daily; he would also know that he could never acquire any foreign language in absolute perfection. Still, he would reach a certain stage in a language, and then he would put it aside and turn to the next one on his programme, and so on. Assuredly, he would not be ashamed of employing method to reach his end.

Now all that can be said of the acquirement of foreign languages can be said of the acquirement of goodwill. In remedying the deficiences of the heart and character, as in remedying the deficiences of mere knowledge, the brain is the sole possible instrument, and the best results will be obtained by using it regularly and scientifically, according to an arranged method. Why, therefore, if a man be proud of method in improving his knowledge, should he see something ridiculous in a deliberate plan for improving his heart—the affair of his heart being immensely more important, more urgent and more difficult? The reader who has found even one good answer to the above question, need read no more of this book, for he will have confounded me and it.

CHAPTER
EIGHT

THE FEAST
OF ST. FRIEND

EIGHT

THE FEAST OF ST. FRIEND

THE consequences of the social self-discipline which I have outlined will be various. A fairly early result will be the gradual decline, and ultimately the death, of the superior person in oneself. It is true that the superior person in oneself has nine lives, and is capable of rising from the dead after even the most fatal blows. But, at worst, the superior person—(and who among us does not shelter that sinister inhabitant in his soul?)—will have a very poor time in the soul of him who steadily practises the imaginative understanding of other people. In the first place, the mere exercise of the imagination on others absolutely scotches egotism as long as it lasts, and leaves it weakened afterwards. And, in the second and more important place, an improved comprehension of others (which means an intensified sympathy with them) must destroy the illusion, so widespread, that one's own case is unique. The amicable study of one's neighbours on the planet inevitably shows that the same troubles, the same fortitudes, the same feats of intelligence, the same successes and failures, are constantly happening everywhere. One can, indeed, see oneself in nearly everybody else, and, in particular, one is struck by the fact that the quality in which one took most pride is simply spread abroad throughout humanity in heaps! It is only in sympathetically contemplating others that one can get

oneself in a true perspective. Yet
probably the majority of human beings
never do contemplate others, save with
the abstracted gaze which proves that
the gazer sees nothing but his own
dream.

*   *   *   *

Another result of the discipline is an
immensely increased interest in one's
friends. One regards them even with
a sort of proprietary interest, for, by
imagination, one has come into sympathetic possession of them. Further,
one has for them that tender feeling
which always follows the conferring of
a benefit, especially the secret conferring of a benefit. It is the benefactor,
not the person benefited, who is grate-
ful. The benefit which one has con-
ferred is, of course, the gift of oneself.
The resulting emotion is independent
of any sympathy rendered by the other;

and where the sympathy is felt to be mutual, friendship acquires a new significance. The exercise of sympathetic imagination will cause one to look upon even a relative as a friend—a startling achievement! It will provide a new excitement and diversion in life.

When the month of December dawns, there need be no sensation of weary apprehension about the difficulty of choosing a present that will suit a friend. Certainly it will not be necessary, from sheer indifference and ignorance, to invite the friend to choose his own present. On the contrary, one will be, in secret, so intimate with the friend's situation and wants and desires, that sundry rival schemes for pleasuring him will at once offer themselves. And when he receives the present finally selected, he will have the conviction, always delightfully flattering to a donee, that he has been the object of a particular attention and insight. * * * And when the cards of greeting are despatched, formal phrases will go forth charged, in the consciousness of the sender, with a genuine meaning, with the force of a climax, as though the sender had written thereon, in invisible ink: "I have had you well in mind during the last twelve months; I think I understand your difficulties and appreciate your efforts better than I did, and so it is with a peculiar sympathetic knowledge that I wish you good luck. I have guessed what particular kind of good luck you require, and I wish accordingly. My wish is not vague and perfunctory only."

*   *   *   *

And on the day of festival itself one feels that one really has something to celebrate. The occasion has a basis, if it had no basis for one before; and if a basis previously existed, then it is widened and strengthened. The festival becomes a public culmination to a private enterprise. One is not reminded by Christmas of goodwill, because the enterprise of imaginative sympathy has been a daily affair throughout the year; but Christmas provides an excuse for taking satisfaction in the success of the enterprise and new enthusiasm to correct its failures. The symbolism of the situation of Christmas, at the turn of the year, develops an added impressiveness, and all the Christmas customs, apt to produce annoyance in the breasts of the unsentimental, are accepted with indulgence, even with eagerness, because their symbolism also is shown in a clearer light. Christmas becomes as personal as a birthday. One eats and drinks to excess, not because it is the custom to eat and drink to excess, but from sheer effervescent faith in an idea. And as one sits with one's friends, possessing them in the privacy of one's heart, permeated by a sense of the value of sympathetic comprehension in this formidable adventure of existence on a planet that rushes eternally through the night of space; assured indeed that companionship and mutual understanding alone make the adventure agreeable,—one sees in a flash that Christmas, whatever else it may be, is and must be the Feast of St. Friend, and a day on that account supreme among the days of the year.

*　　　*　　　*　　　*

The third and greatest consequence of the systematic cultivation of good-

will now grows blindingly apparent.
To state it earlier in all its crudity
would have been ill-advised; and I pur-
posely refrained from doing so. It is
the augmentation of one's own happiness. The increase of amity, the dim-
inution of resentment and annoyance,
the regular maintenance of an attitude
mildly benevolent towards mankind,—
these things are the surest way to happiness. And it is because they are the
surest way to happiness, that the most
enlightened go after them. All real
motives are selfish motives; were it
otherwise humanity would be utterly
different from what it is. A man may
perform some act which will benefit
another while working some striking
injury to himself. But his reason for
doing it is that he prefers the evil of
the injury to the deeper evil of the

fundamental dissatisfaction which would torment him if he did not perform the act. Nobody yet sought the good of another save as a means to his own good. And it is in accordance with common sense that this should be so. There is, however, a lower egotism and a higher. It is the latter which we call unselfishness. And it is the latter of which Christmas is the celebration. We shall legitimately bear in mind, therefore, that Christmas, in addition to being the Feast of St. Friend, is even more profoundly the feast of one's own welfare.

CHAPTER NINE

THE REACTION

NINE

THE REACTION

A REACTION sets in between Christmas and the New Year. It is inevitable; and I should be writing basely if I did not devote to it a full chapter. In those few dark days of inactivity, between a fete and the resumption of the implacable daily round, when the weather is usually cynical, and we are paying in our tissues the fair price of excess, we see life and the world in a grey and sinister light, which we imagine to be the only true light. Take the case of the average successful man of thirty-five. What is he thinking as he lounges about on the day after Christmas?

His thoughts probably run thus: "Even if I live to a good old age, which is improbable, as many years lie behind me as before me. I have lived half my life, and perhaps more than half my life. I have realised part of my worldly ambition. I have made many good resolutions, and kept one or two of them in a more or less imperfect manner. I cannot, as a commonsense person, hope to keep a larger proportion of good resolutions in the future than I have kept in the past. I have tried to understand and sympathise with my fellow creatures, and though I have not entirely failed to do so, I have nearly failed. I am not happy and I am not content. And if, after all these years, I am neither happy nor content, what chance is there of my being happy and content in the second half of my life? The realisation of part of my worldly ambition has not made me any happier, and, therefore, it is unlikely that the realisation of the whole of my ambition will make me any happier. My strength cannot improve; it can only weaken; and my health likewise. I in my turn am coming to believe—what as a youth I rejected with disdain—namely, that happiness is what one is not, and content is what one has not. Why, then, should I go on striving after the impossible? Why should I not let things slide?"

Thus reflects the average successful man, and there is not one of us, successful or unsuccessful, ambitious or unambitious, whose reflections have not often led him to a conclusion equally dissatisfied. Why should I or anybody pretend that this is not so?

*   *   *   *

And yet, in the very moment of his discouragement and of his blackest vision of things, that man knows quite well that he will go on striving. He knows that his instinct to strive will be stronger than his genuine conviction that the desired end cannot be achieved. Positive though he may be that a worldly ambition realised will produce the same dissatisfaction as Dead Sea fruit in the mouth, he will still continue to struggle. * * * Now you cannot argue against facts, and this is a fact. It must be accepted. Conduct must be adjusted to it. The struggle being inevitable, it must be carried through as well as it can be carried through. It will not end brilliantly, but precautions can be taken against it ending disgracefully. These precautions consist in the devising of a plan of campaign, and the plan of campaign is defined by a series of resolutions: which resolutions are generally made at or immediately before the beginning of a New Year. Without these the struggle would be formless, confused, blind and even more futile than it is with them. Organised effort is bound to be less ineffective than unorganised effort.

*   *   *   *

A worldly ambition can be, frequently is, realised: but an ideal cannot be attained—if it could, it would not be an ideal. The virtue of an ideal is its unattainability. It seems, when it is first formed, just as attainable as a worldly ambition which indeed is often schemed as a means to it. After twenty-four hours, the ideal is all but attained. After forty-eight, it is a little farther off. After a week, it has receded still further. After a month it is far away; and towards the end of a year even the keen eye of hope has almost lost sight of it; it is definitely withdrawn from the practical sphere. And then, such is the divine obstinacy of humanity, the turn of the year gives us an excuse for starting afresh, and forming a new ideal, and forgetting our shame in yet another organised effort. Such is the annual circle of the ideal, the effort, the failure and the shame. A rather pitiful history it may appear! And yet it is also rather a splendid history! For the failure and the shame are due to the splendour of our ideal and to the audacity of our faith in ourselves. It is only in comparison with our ideal that we have fallen low. We are higher, in our failure and our shame, than we should have been if we had not attempted to rise.

*   *   *   *

There are those who will say: "At any rate, we might moderate somewhat the splendour of our ideal and the audacity of our self-conceit, so that there should be a less grotesque disparity between the aim and the achievement. Surely such moderation would be more in accord with common sense! Surely it would lessen the spiritual fatigue and disappointment caused by sterile endeavour!" It would. But just try to moderate the ideal and the self-conceit! And you will find, in spite of all your sad experiences, that you cannot. If there is the stuff of a man in you, you

[103]

simply cannot! The truth is that, in
the supreme things, a man does not act
under the rules of earthly common
sense. He transcends them, because
there is a quality in him which compels
him to do so. Common sense may per-
suade him to attempt to keep down the
ideal, and self-conceit may pretend to
agree. But all the time, self-conceit
will be whispering: "I can go one better than that." And lo! the ideal is
furtively raised again.

A man really has little scientific con-
trol over the height of his ideal and the
intensity of his belief in himself. He
is born with them, as he is born with a
certain pulse and a certain reflex ac-
tion. He can neglect the ideal, so that
it almost dissolves, but he cannot
change its height. He can maim his
belief in himself by persistent abandon-

ment to folly, but he cannot lower its
flame by an effort of the will, as he
might lower the flame of a gas by a
calculated turn of the hand. In the
secret and inmost constitution of humanity it is ordained that the disparity
between the aim and the achievement
shall seem grotesque; it is ordained that
there shall be an enormous fuss about
pretty nearly nothing; it is ordained
that the mountain shall bring forth a
mouse. But it is also ordained that men
shall go blithely on just the same, ignor-
ing in practice the ridiculousness which
they admit in theory, and drawing renewed hope and conceit from some
magic, exhaustless source. And this is
the whole philosophy of the New Year's
resolution.

CHAPTER TEN

ON THE LAST DAY OF THE YEAR

TEN

ON THE LAST DAY OF THE YEAR

THERE are few people who arrive at a true understanding of life, even in the calm and disillusioned hours of reflection that come between the end of one annual period and the beginning of another. Nearly everybody has an idea at the back of his head that if only he could conquer certain difficulties and embarrassments, he might really start to live properly, in the full sense of living. And if he has pluck he says to himself: "I *will* smooth things out, and then I'll really live." In the same way, nearly everybody, regarding the spectacle of the world, sees therein a principle which he calls Evil; and he thinks: "If only we could get rid of this Evil, if only we could set things right, how splendid the world would be!" Now, in the meaning usually attached to it, there is no such positive principle as Evil. Assuming that there is such a positive principle in a given phenomenon—such as the character of a particular man—you must then admit that there is the same positive principle everywhere, for just as the character of no man is so imperfect that you could not conceive a worse, so the character of no man is so perfect that you could not conceive a better. Do away with Evil from the world, and you would not merely abolish certain specially distressing matters, you would change everything. You would in fact achieve perfection. And when we say that one thing is evil and another good, all that we mean is that one thing is less advanced than another in the way of perfection. Evil cannot therefore be a positive principle; it signifies only the falling short of perfection.

And supposing that the desires of mankind were suddenly fulfilled, and the world was rendered perfect! There would be no motive for effort, no alteration of conflicting motives in the human heart; nothing to do, no one to befriend, no anxiety, no want unsatisfied. Equilibrium would be established. A cheerful world! You can see instantly how amusing it would be. It would have only one drawback—that of being dead. Its reason for being alive would have ceased to operate. Life means change through constant development. But you cannot develop the perfect. The perfect can merely expire.

That average successful man whom I have previously cited feels all this by instinct, though he does not comprehend it by reason. He reaches his ambition, and retires from the fight in order to enjoy life,—and what does he then do? He immediately creates for himself a new series of difficulties and embarrassments, either by undertaking the management of a large estate, or by some other device. If he does not maintain for himself conditions which necessitate some kind of struggle, he quickly dies—spiritually or physically, often both. The proportion of men who, having established an equilibrium, proceed to die on the spot, is enormous. Continual effort, which means, of course, continual disappointment, is the *sine qua non*—without it there is literally nothing vital. Its abolition is the abolition of life. Hence, people, who, failing to savour the struggle itself, anticipate the end of the struggle as the beginning of joy and happiness—these people are simply missing life; they are longing to exchange life for death. The hemlock would save them a lot of weary waiting.

*   *   *   *

We shall now perceive, I think, what is wrong with the assumptions of the average successful man as set forth in the previous chapter. In postulating that happiness is what one is not, he has got hold of a mischievous conception of happiness. Let him examine his conception of happiness, and he will find that it consists in the enjoyment of love and luxury, and in the freedom from enforced effort. He generally wants all three ingredients. Now passionate love does not mean happiness; it means excitement, apprehension and continually renewed desire. And affectionate love, from which the passion has faded, means something less than happiness, for, mingled with its gentle tranquility is a disturbing regret for the more fiery past. Luxury, according to the universal experience of those who have had it, has no connection whatever with happiness. And as for freedom from enforced effort, it means simply death.

Happiness as it is dreamed of cannot possibly exist save for brief periods of self-deception which are followed by terrible periods of reaction. Real, practicable happiness is due primarily not to any kind of environment, but to an inward state of mind. Real happiness consists first in acceptance of the

fact that discontent is a condition of
life, and, second, in an honest endeavour to adjust conduct to an ideal. Real
happiness is not an affair of the future;
it is an affair of the present. Such as
it is, if it cannot be obtained now, it can
never be obtained. Real happiness
lives in patience, having comprehended
that if very little is accomplished towards perfection, so a man's existence
is a very little moment in the vast ex-
panse of the universal life, and having
also comprehended that it is the struggle which is vital, and that the end of
the struggle is only another name for
death.

*   *   *   *

"Well," I hear you exclaiming, "if
this is all we can look forward to, if this
is all that real, practicable happiness
amounts to, is life worth living?" That

is a question which each person has to answer for himself. If he answers it in the negative, no argument, no persuasion, no sentimentalisation of the facts of life, will make him alter his opinion. Most people, however, answer it in the affirmative. Despite all the drawbacks, despite all the endless disappointments, they decide that life is worth living. There are two species of phenomena which bring them to this view. The first may be called the golden moments of life, which seem somehow in their transient brevity to atone for the dull exasperation of interminable mediocre hours: moments of triumph in the struggle, moments of fierce exultant resolve; moments of joy in nature—moments which defy oblivion in the memory, and which, being priceless, cannot be too dearly bought.

THE FEAST OF ST. FRIEND

The second species of compensatory phenomena are all the agreeable experiences connected with human friendship; the general feeling, under diverse forms, that one is not alone in the world. It is for the multiplication and intensification of these phenomena that Christmas, the Feast of St. Friend, exists. And, on the last day of the year, on the eve of a renewed effort, our thoughts may profitably be centered upon a plan of campaign whose execution shall result in a less imperfect intercourse.